I, Too, Bloom

I, Too, Bloom

A Poetry Collection

LAURA SERRATOS

Copyright © 2021 I, too, bloom.

All rights reserved. No part of this publication may be reproduced, distributed ut the prior written permission of the publisher, except in the case of brief quotations embodied in critical reviews and certain other noncommercial uses permitted by copyright law. For permission requests, write to the publisher, addressed "Attention: Permissions Coordinator," at the e-mail address below.

davina@alegriamagazine.com

Library of Congress Control Number: 2021907605

ISBN: 9781736149638

Published by Alegria Publishing
Book cover and layout by Sirenas Creative

Foreword

When we met, she lived across the hall and seemed quiet. Her dark hair and eyes seemed to keep her secrets. Her smile though, her smile hid nothing. Once she smiled, it was as if you had never seen anyone smile before, like seeing the most beautiful and brightest sunrise.

At first, we were just hallway neighbors, but slowly we merged into friends. We found commonalities that created a bond. We were both Latina, both teachers, both parents, and both strong women with creative souls.

She had the best laugh. She would often come into my classroom and we'd talk and laugh to remove ourselves from the chaos of our classes. She had a sense of humor and a giggle that would make even the cutest little girl jealous. Sometimes I would go into her classroom to vent; she was good at listening.

Our classrooms were across the hall from each other, but then we became more than hallway neighbors, we became neighborhood neighbors, too. With our backyards now facing each other, we would laugh and giggle the way school girls do when they have secret crushes. She told me about the dreams she had; some of the secrets that her eyes and dark hair had been harboring.

She demands more from life. She wants to embrace it and squeeze the air out of it. In her life, she has worn many hats: daughter, sister, wife, mother, grandmother, teacher, and friend, but she is even more than all of these. She is a traveler, a writer, and a poet and her words are her oxygen .

Laura Serratos writes with a pen that holds her soul. She strokes the paper with words that allows you to escape and give you your freedom like a curvy old country road. Her poems are like invitations to the secrets she harbors in her dark eyes and hair.

      I'm proud of Laura for being proud enough of all the hats she wears. She has put all of those characteristics into words for all of us to find our own passions and ultimately ourselves.

      Her words and her poetry are a beacon of light in a world where daughters, sisters, wives, mothers, grandmothers, teachers, friends, travelers, writers, and sometimes, even poets, are still afraid to pour out their souls. Laura found life in a pen and courage in her heart to dream, to write, and to give the rest of us a voice to speak the secrets that we harbor.

-Angela M. Herrera, Teacher, mother, wife, dreamer

Preface

I remember, as an eight year old girl, I spent many weekends in that weathered house on Brandon Ave in the South Chicago neighborhood. My grandparents' home was a mecca for fun and creativity. This was where I lovingly assembled my first handmade book and my dream of being an author.

There are few other ways that calm my heart and soul as does writing. I knew as a child that putting my feelings into a lockable Holly Hobbie diary would make things better. In my personal, adult life, journaling has been a lifesaver. As therapy for sorting out my feelings, writing has been an integral part of who I was, who I am, and who I am becoming.

I was formally introduced to poetry when I took an English course in college. Neither Emily Dickinson, William Shakespeare, nor Walt Whitman resonated with me after the first read, but there was something special about poetry in which I just could not put my finger on at the time. Nevertheless, poetry made an impression on me and would eventually make its way into my heart. Faced with questioning what I intended to do to make my own mark in my world, I began to write poetry. I had no idea how or when this would come to fruition. However, I wrote poetry in my spare time. It was a way to disguise feelings and emotions I was not ready to openly share.

Hardly a day had gone by that I did not think about writing a book of my own. I had made many attempts in the past at short stories and novels which would get lost in the shuffle of motherhood, classroom holiday parties and Girl Scout events. However, I knew deep in my soul that I would someday make this dream a reality.

Six months prior to the publication of this book, I struggled with trying to create an eBook. Synchronistically,

I, Too, Bloom

I came upon the opportunity to legitimately put my words to print. In a time when many people were suffering and unsure of how to spend their days, I had taken control and finally put my time and energy into a tangible manifestation of my idea. One that not only comprises what I considered personal and deep emotions but has given me a true vision of my own growth as a writer, author, and poet. This book journey has been essential to the growth I had been experiencing in all areas of my life. Through a self-imposed writing challenge, I was able to draw out many hidden experiences -sometimes painful, sometimes joyful- to write from my heart and soul. In retrospect, there is not a thing I would change in the process of writing that went into the production of this book. My goal is to inspire my readers with beautifully written, thought provoking words and themes. I am now ready and happy to share bits of myself, still saving some for the next project waiting to come to life.

Laura Serratos

I, Too, Bloom

"Sometimes words and thoughts can be prepackaged
   -neat little gifts
      -given to the world
         -to unwrap and nurture
Like seeds in a paper packet"

-Laura Serratos

Laura Serratos

This is Me

Sometimes I feel broken, sad, alone
Like an outcast I have been left behind
But there's nothing wrong with me

Sometimes I feel nervous, anxious, uneasy
Like I can't stand to be in my own skin
But there's nothing wrong with me

Sometimes I feel helpless, hopeless, scared
Like the weight of the word is crushing
But there's nothing wrong with me

Sometimes I feel invisible, worthless, useless
Like I have no reason to live this life
But there's nothing wrong with me

At times I feel valued, appreciated, loved
Like I am the center of everyone's life
So there must be something wrong with me

At times I feel strong, brave, ready
Like nothing can stop my dreams
So there must be something wrong with me

At times I feel excited, joyful, happy
Like my soul is free and unchained
So there must be something wrong with me

At times I freely give, care, love
Like my heart is bursting with emotions
So, there must be something wrong with me

This is me

The Depths of My Heart

Beating with every passing moment
      marks the depth of my heart's endearment

Flowing like a river through time
      carries my heart's blood of crime

Supplying life to each broken part
      ensures my heart's scars never depart

Removing pain from one chamber to the next
      creates my heart's memories so complex

Searching through fragile pieces sifted apart
      opens up the depth of my heart

In My Dreams

When darkness falls at day's end,
                my mind searches its depths

to know before the sun shines
to understand across time
to feel past pain and misery
to believe for a brief moment,

        I am more than the aching memories
that shadow over peaceful rest.

What Did You See?

You saw me walk in, I guess I was a threat.
You saw a girl with brown hair, brown eyes, fair skin.
You saw a spawn; two little girls the mirror image of me

You saw a foreign culture; primitive, inferior, dirty
You saw a burden on society; poor, deprived, lacking

You were disgusted beyond stares which pierced my soul.
Your anger, fueled by hate, provoked you to see a girl of little value to this world.

Your words were louder than any sound that could ring through my ears, harder than any blow.

You did not see a woman five generations worth trying to live a happy life.
You did not see a mother raising good, respectful daughters who would rise above your low expectations.
You did not see Mexican pride at its finest contributing to the beauty of this world.

An educated Latina
An English teacher
A Writer
A Poet

Still, I carry your anger and hate with me.

My burning eyes and voice aflame yearning to shout
"You don't know what you see!"

The Judgement

Her cold stares piercing hatefully hard,
    The wrinkled eyes fixed on my appearance,
    The aged woman disgusted by my young existence,
She judged my character
        Across the table
        through soulless glances
        in a taut voice
        of hateful words
        about my culture and
        of my worth in this world.

Her lack of judgement weighing strong,
    The misconceptions spewed at four generations,
    The aged woman determined to belittle me,
She would never see
        before her an educated woman
        within the heart of a mother
        from a prideful Latina stance
        to this day
        by means of anger and hostility
        inside the scar I carry forever.

Head to Toe

My head provides space to dream. I dream of another life.

My face becomes a canvas to display. I display a lifetime of worry.

My eyes reflect pain to see. I see a life without chains.

My lips pulse in hunger to kiss. I kiss soft, tender moments.

My voice longs to shout. I shout a whisper of hope.

My shoulders give strength to carry. I carry the weight of my soul.

My neck meant to stretch. I stretch beyond the limits of patience.

My chin turns up to uphold. I uphold pride towards a higher place.

My chest beats with a heart to love. I love with a spirit of joy.

My breasts fill with strength to nourish. I nourish the next generation.

My arms reach out to embrace. I embrace memories from a lifetime ago.

My hands clasp tightly to hold. I hold moments in the palm of my hands.

My legs struggle to stand. I stand taller than the walls built around me.

My feet yearn to run. I run towards a dream.

My body was born to be; I am a woman, head to toe.

A Young Heart

What does a young heart behold?
  One, not yet blinded
    by scorn, jealousy, strain

What does a young heart embrace?
  One, not yet rejected
    by hurt, loss, pain

What does a young heart heed?
  One, not yet deafened
    by ridicule, judgement, screams

What does a young heart savor?
  One, not yet tainted
    by ash, dew, fear

What does a young heart relish?
  One, not yet bitter
    by blood, toil, tears

A young heart not cherished
  will one day perish

A young heart made numb
will someday succumb

A Moment of Pleasure

A moment of pleasure
flows over like rain
As thoughts arise to measure
    a lifetime of pain

A secret worth keeping
    Shared only by tears
A notion endearing
    Kept hidden for years

An instance of release
    Never meant to feel
A sensation of peace
    Purify and heal

A point in time now lost
    from struggles within
Hoping for love at costs
    of heartache and sin

My Uniqueness

My uniqueness blends two cultures
Distinct traits from a pair of subcultures
American born between bilateral borders
Mexican heritage held in high honor
Two worlds within this waking woman

My uniqueness blends two cultures
with an accent which sounds uncultured
English is mother to my mouth
Spanish sounds foreign and forgotten
R's don't roll rhythmically from my tongue

My uniqueness blends two cultures
Cuisine devours my taste buds like vultures
Pizza, potato chips, pickles, American pie, or
Tacos, tostadas, tamales typical Mexican treats
Savory choices for this Coconut's cravings

My uniqueness blends two cultures
Faith grown on white and brown sculptures
Hail Mary, Mother of my Catholic soul
Our Lady of Guadalupe give me grace
Heaven, cielo, hell, infierno–Where will I go?

My uniqueness blends two cultures
Identity built around different structures
Skyscrapers and sidewalks serenade the scene
The old country perceived only in my mind
A foreigner in either homeland

My uniqueness blends two cultures
Brown eyed girl may cause a rupture
Too fair among the ancestors
Too brown in the midst of milky whiteness
Two worlds arising within this waking woman

Laura Serratos

Love Marooned

My thoughts slowly drift
through an ocean of memories
My heart floating on waves
of sadness and regret
My soul searching for light
across mystifying dark waters
My spirit washed ashore, tangled
in knots of love marooned

Butterflies

Soft, powdery wings
Heaven's angels watching me
Bringing love and light

Goddess

Natural
Oval tan curves
Rough around the edges
Leave me alone, I'm loose and free
Need warmth

Growing Goddess

Spirit
White roots flourish
Green stems and striped vein leaves
Hold my stem with love, free of weeds
Cool Spring

Green Goddess

Yellow
Sugar coated
Creator with the wind
Woman celebrates life and death
Emerge

Green Goddess Rising

One touch
Young, green, and ripe
Open and mature seed
Green Goddess heals over time
Rising

Laura Serratos

Passion

Beautiful, yet strange
Delicate, yet strong
Tightly embraced
Easily taken
Lost to time
Found in pain

Sole Survivor

Where do you think *you're* going, girl?
You didn't even ask if you could leave
You just grab me and buff me on your sleeve
Never stop to think, in your rushed little whirl
that I might have a say in how you step or twirl
Do I align today with what the fashion gods believe?
or do you try to pass me off as a match that I can't perceive?
Am I too plain, should I have come in a pattern or swirl?

Do you even notice my strength?
What color of my soul do you see?
I am much more durable than you know
I've been around for quite the length
I guess I should be grateful, you picked *me*
So wherever you go, I will unquestionably glow

Velvet Box

My mind is filled with trinkets
Tucked away memories of the past
Precious jewels I never thought would last
Emotions wrapped around like bracelets
Bound feelings of shackled anklets
What's kept inside gives contrast
to the reminders that are vast
among multidimensional facets

Gems that tell tales of old
Gifts commemorate the new
My mind searches through the heap
longing to make statements bold
Diamond confessions that ring true
Soft velvet depths, where time keeps

Handle With Care

Your shoulder, always there for me
Your body securely next to mine
Leather skin, delicate and fine
wrapped in loving glee
Never let me slip away free
I am with you as a sign
that together we dazzle and shine
Worn from a life carefree

I hold your beauty within
I understand your worth
I'm not a beat up bag
You toss me with a sly grin
I hope you have a rebirth
when you behold my swag

New Moon

Between two places
Filling voided spaces
Beauty not seen
Thoughts become clean
removing negative traces

Waxing Gibbous

Growing by light
Half goddess in sight
Fresh goals set
For things yet met
Mindful of a creative night

Full Moon

Flowing with illumination
Release all intention
Growth by soul
Seal spiritual goal
Inward gratification

Waning Gibbous

Intentions look inward
Thoughts move forward
Grateful at heart
Reflections impart
Thankfulness aimed skyward

Water

Crystal energy
affirm my longing within
quench my doubting soul

Earth

Aquamarine stone
swirled among glass oceans
of abundant life

Air

Invisible breath
blow gentle whispers of
everlasting life

Fire

Consuming passion
golden amber blazes rise
inflamed by desire

Laura Serratos

I, Too, Bloom

"Poetry should come from your heart,
       where its energy can reach someone.
If it only comes from your head, it might go without passion."

-Laura Serratos

Laura Serratos

At My Cafe

Beyond milestone moments
in beautiful Nola
under illusions of time
during a December morning

Despite chilly misty sprinkles
among the melodious Big Easy
within French market frenzy
on streets of Bourbon spirits

For a hot coffee with milk
of chicory scents
with pillowy fried dough
amid dusty sugar air

Above "Merry Little Christmas" melodies
through a tarnished brass sax
outside entertaining street musician
over the line of sleepy travelers

Beyond perfect notes of cheer
between purple and turquoise dreams
down a road of delightful memories
to a sweet paradise of French delicacies

Autumn

New beginnings
reveal vivid melodies of creativity
Golden brown leaves sway to the wind
gently fall to the earth

Winter

Powdery flakes,
on blades and crisp leaves, blanket forgotten creation
Giving hope to a sleepy sprout
of vibrant beginnings

Spring

Fresh growth
Blooming colors dance with iridescent rainbows
roaring loudly behind a gentle lamb
as warm rainy days dry in the sun

Summer

Endless days
of sunbaked beauties and cozy evenings
become faint childhood memories
when the ninth month beckons a new dawn

Laura Serratos

Night Sky

Deep blue dream
blanket the night
with diamond light
Drifting clouds
pass over velvet
shades of sapphire
Lost in sight
of traveling stars
and stunning views

Miracles

Mysterious
tiny miracles
give birth to
new ways of cherishing
life

Wounds

Wounds are meant to heal
Can't help but not want to feel
The process is full of strain
Aches that hold pain
They say you just need time
Don't pay them mind
Learn from all the hurt
But it feels like infected dirt
These wounds might be a gift
Once the pain my spirits lift

Alluring Luna

Pure white light
    beams from your beauty

Silvery clouds shadow and
    overcast your charm

As floating diamonds cross
    a rich glittery sky
unexpected emotions stir
    as silver energy intensifies

Darkness gives luminosity
    to deep blemishes of time passed

Heavenly body scarred and sacred
    among a sparkling presence

Brilliance outshines the stars'
    phase of infatuation

Cycle of desire eclipsed
    by Alluring Luna

Pink Desires

Close your eyes for a moment...

> Satin ribbons dance in your mind
> Desires from the heart arise
> Porcelain dreams of rosy cheeks
> Skates cruising over pavement
> Boy crush endlessly out of reach
> An angel baby of your own
> Freedom from a lifeless existence
> A spirit on fire with energy
> A soul to transcend time
> A place among the stars

Inhale love...
      ...exhale hope

of a young girl's
pink wishes

Kiss of Winter

Crisp, white coated grass. Frosty dark evenings.
Wind howls with a chilled voice. Icy prints on windows.
Scratch and make ice crystals under eager fingernails.
Treats for a new season. Hot chocolate, peppermint candy,
multicolored lights flicker in the iridescence of billowy
snowflakes.
Arrive too soon and leave in a hurry. Joy to the world
and the year to come. Memories made once again.
Indelible sting on my cheek. Rosy pink perfection
of winter's kiss.

Musings of A Woman

Beautiful, sexy woman
Sultry energy permeates the world
Glistening eyes mesmerize with a glance
Parted soft lips invite tender kisses
Cocoa butter scents flow over silky skin
Feminine curves entice a longing embrace
Magical charm attracts mindful souls
Tempting seductive smile casts spells
Mirrors distort true personas
Subconscious musings reveal
        what the world will now perceive

A beautiful, sexy woman

Liberation

Liberating a woman
        Terrifying to her mind

Giving her thoughts of
        Exploring space and time

Flying through the years
        Gliding across the sky

Expanding her wings
        Preparing to take flight

Keeping her grounded
        Becoming impossible to try

Laura Serratos

Sidewalk

Broken
hearts endlessly
bear wounds like
cracks in the sidewalk
Forever

Winter Morning

Dark
cold morning
winds rejuvenate my
soul and invigorate my
spirits

Snowy Nights

sparkly
flaky
icy
slushy

Blowing flaky dreams on sparkly nights
      bring slushy thoughts across icy lights

Butterfly Sky

Misty
Mighty
Happy
Rosy

Floating through a misty, rosy sky
      mighty angels in happy paths fly

Yummy Kiss

Creamy
Silky
Yummy
Heavenly

Touch of creamy, silky addiction
        A yummy heavenly temptation

Healing Hearts

Spoken
Taken
Broken
Given

A spoken lie to a taken heart
        A given myth forms a broken start

Mistletoe Bliss

Grateful
Hopeful
Faithful
Joyful

Two grateful lips bond in joyful bliss
      Faithful souls create a hopeful kiss

Laura Serratos

Citrus Sky

Morning
tangerine sky
refresh my senses
with luscious canvases of
citrus

Mija, Are You Ok?

Are you ok, mija?
is what my Mana would say
Her sweet words of comfort
in my mind now stay

What did she see at the time?
Was it my flesh that looked in pain?
Was my soul transparent?
or did my spirit cry out with strain?

This question I now ask of myself
Mija, are you ok?
I reflect deeply within my soul
and write the pain away

This question so essential
to explore feelings hard to describe
and ponder what stirs inside me
But not always a negative vibe

Lately I've been healing
self-doubt and fear
My mindset has been changing
getting closer to a life that's pure

So, are you ok, Mija?
Her words simple yet fierce
heals where my heart's been pierced

Laura Serratos

Dear Stone

In the palm
of my hand
dear stone,

you fulfill
my dreams and
deep wishes

Pure beauty,
your power
so cosmic

If vast charm
flows within
your small form,

imagine
the power,
within me!

If ...

If there were no darkness, I would not have found light
If there were no pain, I would not need to heal
If there were no fear, I would not need to be brave
If there were no doubt, I would have no reason to believe
If there were nothing to lose, I would not have taken a chance
If I had all the strength, I would not seek courage
If I had everything I wanted, I would not feel gratitude in my heart
If I had taken nothing for granted, I would not be able to give thanks
If I had everything guaranteed, I would not know tireless effort
If times were not rough, I would not cherish smooth days
If there were no chaos, I would not seek calm.

If I had not inhaled hate, I would not have exhaled love

Laura Serratos

I, Too, Bloom

"If you see a sprout, water it
        nurture it,
        encourage it,
        love it,
just as a feeling needs to be encouraged to continue to grow
        into something worthy and beautiful."

-*Laura Serratos*

Laura Serratos

Selene in Sorrow

She wanders through the night
through shadows cast by her light
    searching for signs of lost love.

Moonbeam tears glistening bright
Illuminated sorrow flowing in sight
    falling graceful from sunken eyes

Agnes, Where Are You?

Always waiting in the wings
behind the curtain too long
Pages of a scripted life
A memorized existence
practiced night and day
Emotions arise at once
        nervous
        excited
        scared
        anxious
        happy
        joy
        satisfaction
        triumph
The curtain draws back
Enter stage left of reality
A performance of a lifetime
Ready to make an appearance
the world eagerly awaits

Agnes, where are you?

Medallion

1940's silver peso
Valued only by my heart
handcrafted memories
A lovely crescent moon
An etched token of love
Honoring Our Lady
above radiance and light
Left as a remembrance
of a lifetime ago
Sentimental moments which live
in our thoughts and words
Family defined not by flesh
but the core of my soul

Laura Serratos

Sleepless Mind

My body is tired
but my mind wants conversation
2 am thoughts persist
Why can't this wait 'til morning?
I'll be fresh and new...Ready
But then how will I hear?
Will these ramblings make sense?
A new day brings distractions
Night time is quiet
Yes, quiet for rest
No, silent for listening
Listening to gloomy chatter
I don't want to entertain these thoughts
I try to exhaust my body by day
but a bed of lies awaits
My mind is ready...Ready
to hear the questions which play again
Don't engage with answers
Don't give in with quick agreement
These conversations bring no peace
They have no place but in a weary mind
Trapped in a tired body
the days are good and flowing
Yes, the days bring joy
but the night needs reconciling
Until I face my fears
the night belongs to insecurities and
a sleepless mind

Genie in a Bottle

Life in a glass house
no one sees my true self
From the outside, the walls
iridescent purple and pink
smooth to the touch
Its beauty attracts many hands
but it's not easy to hold
From inside, the walls reveal a clear world
Stares of wonder make my heart leap
Massage me free, please
I want to soar among the stars
but I'm swaying in a bottle
I long for freedom
Still, I resist with all my might
I have a million questions to ask
The crystal stopper keeps my voice unheard
I'll rest in my rosy velvet space
waiting to rise like burning incense
My glass house is safe
That's why it exists
Am I transparent to you?
Even if you let me out
I'll find my way back inside
Maybe once the earth rotates the sun
you will see my power
Feel my love

Laura Serratos

Dream

I envision a dream world
That is where you belong
I feel your presence
Sometimes I feel your touch
Your lips on my forehead
My lips search for yours
but you draw back
You can't give more
So I pull away
even if my heart breaks
As I accept the loneliness
You give just enough
to bring me back
longing for your touch once more
My eyes swell with tears
that I refuse to let pour
My chest tightens in pain
at the thought of your resistance
You keep me close
but your gentle push hurts
more than a shove
I think you like this game
So I'll continue to play
Not showing my true face
I smile at your indifference
I embrace your carelessness
Because you are my dream

Soul Searching

This place seems familiar
Have we been here before?
What are we looking for?
I search every room
You are here with me
I can feel you around me
Your voice is soundless
I feel your words
You crave freedom
I do too
We are trapped
by each other's needs
I need assurance
You need safety
I need purpose
You need pride
Our chains to each other
grow closer by the day
I give you hope
You bring me peace
We embrace for a moment
among disapproving eyes
We don't make sense
yet our bond embodies soundness
Two souls seeking through the depths
of each other's misery

Laura Serratos

Alley of Dreams

Darkness consumes this place
Light is only deep within our souls
Moving toward a woman
her young child close
Standing among a wasteland
of familiar childhood surroundings
yet a place never seen
Watching youthful spirits rise
through weeds and rubble
Midnight falls upon our senses
a nervous hand on her shoulder
gives a gentle touch
We feel safe and protected
Three souls come together
The power among them cosmic
Black garments reflect the moonlight
and dimming street lamps
It's time to go home
Ponder a strange encounter
with a struggling survivor
in the alleyway of time
Paved with memories
trash cans, weeds, and stone
We've been here before
We will return again

Unworthy

Why was I not worthy
of love and attention?
Was it my hair,
my face,
my skin,
my untimely birth?
You looked through me as if I did not exist.
Did I not meet your expectations?
I was just a child
I was not at fault for your insecurities and sins
I could not control circumstances
Who I came from should not have mattered
but it did
I was the first
treated like the last
Trapped in the middle by
your looks of cold indifference
your hugs of forced emotions
I was never good enough
Yet I paid the price
Years have gone by so quickly
I should be by your side now
You're so close to the end
but you sealed our fate
I guess once you're gone
I'll be free
Worthy

Laura Serratos

Darkness Falls

Darkness falls
on this bright memory
Black and gray scenes
play out in front of my eyes
Gloomy days and scary nights
do not exist in my cherished home
I long to go back
just a fantasy now
I feel the pangs of joy
when I see this place
I wander the dark streets
I know where I am going
but I can't seem to find my way
It gets further from my grasp
Why is it so shocking?
No color
No sound
The stillness scares me
yet this place brings comfort
I want to stay here
What will happen if I leave?
This is where I need to live
My mind longs for the feelings
though I awake once more

My Path

I walk this path alone
picking up stones along the way
marking phases of time
Each one in my hand
brings me inner peace
As I pick up a new stone,
a pebble of my past drops away from me
I collect a clear white stone
bringing me new life
as I release self-doubt and fear
A golden orange heart ignites my words
as I let go of shame and hesitancy
I struggle to share this walk
my secret heart's journey
I was led here by silence
I was left here by indifference
I reach inside the mesh sac once again
feeling the energy of these stones in my hand
and set intentions for my journey
Kicking gravel around my feet
I hope to choose wisely
asking for guidance on this road
If others should walk behind me
I pray they don't pick up water worn
remnants of tainted memories

Magic Wand

My pen is a magic wand
scripting a new story of my life
Black river flowing gently
soaking paper, earth, and sky
My thoughts become words
My words become images
My desires set for eternity

My pen creates an original reality
manifesting beauty and freedom
Mornings set peaceful intentions
penciling out limiting beliefs and lies

My pen invents a fresh woman
journaling a cascade of affirmations
meant to heal and cure
Bringing life in a novel direction

My pen eagerly awaits the world
inscribing a legacy for loved ones
Creations dreamily haunt their minds
eternally analyzing my words

My pen is a magic wand
Composing immortalized emotions
Forever casting notions
without melody, reason, or rhyme

More Than Grand

He was my rock
The strength I needed
He gave so much more
than he had ever thought of taking
He gave up his dreams
to make mine come true
This soul could have held
the universe in his hands
but he chose to live in my world
with love and happiness

He could have flown among the stars
but he chose to remain grounded
This spirit, who painted masterpieces
chose to sketch cartoons on Saturday morning

He could have climbed mountains
but he chose to take walks in the park
This man, who had a major league hand
chose to play catch in the backyard

Grand is not good enough to describe
the heart and soul of this man
who had many titles from which to choose
but he chose "grandfather"

Life Lost

Where did life go?
I'm sure I was here
I allowed time to slip
through my fearful hands

Yesterday I was walking
to the bus stop with my backpack.
I can't be late again
but that happens when no one
seems to care how you make it.
My imagination kept time
I starved myself from food
when what I craved was attention

Did I really let a boy replace the man?
The one who should have held my hand
I guess this is where life lost
to the hands of time

Turning Point

I let this happen
I wanted validation but
feelings spun out of control
along with hormones

If I could do it all again
I would be a little smarter
That's what I tell myself anyway
I had too much freedom
I didn't respect its power
So it was taken away
Now my body and youth
would pay the dear price

I had dreams
I had hopes
Was it not enough?
What magic did I reveal?
I long to be her again
the authentic younger me
I would hold her tight to my chest
turn her face away from his charms
cover her with love
protect her with confidence
Fluff her wings in preparation
to take flight among the stars
and resist the moment
that would change her forever

Love, Laura G.

Dear Laura B,

It's December. Your birth month. Your season of joy. You will not believe where you are. Slowly the life of your dreams unfolding.

You are at a point in time that you will forever cherish. Make the most of your playful days.

You need to know a few things. Believe every word I write here. I have already lived it. You chose a path, a lonely path, but you are never alone. You feel left behind, but you catch up. You do things you swore you would never do, but you know how to spin the truth.

There will be twists and turns, detours and shortcuts, but they lead to a genuine place. Never lose hope. You encounter rough patches and heartache. You inspire the world. You are guided by butterflies and protected by creation. God carries you!

Love, Laura S.

Fashion Doll Dreams

Take my hand
I have a surprise
Your favorite place
where pink walls wrap
canopies of white lace
A place safe for imagination
Soft plush carpet comforts
a collection of porcelain dolls
Delightful dresses drape a closet
A hideaway of make believe
and abandoned fashion dolls
Once the center of your world
Let's dress them up
Let's give them a voice
Yours and mine
They don't look like us
but we don't mind
This is just make believe
This is just for fun
In real life
our image magnifies

My Heart

My heart still beats for you
in a steady rhythm
Like pearls dropping from a string
and tapping gently on the floor
You never left my heart
Your substance fills a chamber
just hidden for some time
I think about you often
more lately than ever before
I moved ahead of you
You stopped trying to catch up
My pace grew stronger as if
trying to leave you in the past
We should have stayed together
hand in hand throughout time
I search for you now
Every beat of my heart
is a thought of you
I'll break through that chamber
to find you once again
Hold you in my arms
Keep you by my side
The world might judge us
We'll pay them no mind
because with a steady rhythm
my heart still beats for you

A Sign

Give me sign
Is this for me?
A path of destiny
Waiting for me
Eyes focused on the goal
Like a hawk searching
for its nourishment
I rub this crystal
in my anxious hands
waiting for the words
to flow like a river
Ripples of time
across my hands
Fingers tossing gently
satisfying smooth touch
My energy high
with my warmth
Beautiful words
flowing from ink
and a mind's well
Like a hollow ditch
waiting to be filled
with love
Affirmations
Validation

Laura Serratos

Sky on Fire

The sky is aflame
burning for love
Swelled with passion

A ripple of sensation
flows through the trees
waiting for desires
to be fanned
by a caressing wind
Even the clouds part
allowing a pleasurable breeze

The sky is aflame
with unstoppable heat
reddish-yellow waves
scorching a lustful prey
Consuming what passes through
The sky bonded now with
the raging sun

I, Too, Bloom

Laura Serratos

I, Too, Bloom

"You might not expect the growth you made to set the world on fire, but your own world will burst into flames."

-Laura Serratos

Laura Serratos

Reflection Speaks

Waking up is easy
Minds never rest
The mirror her first encounter
with the one she must face
Not knowing what she feels
until the reflection speaks
She stares outside the window
a portal to a futuristic reality
reflecting on life, love
All the things that matter
All the things that don't
The morning moon crescent
a sliver of hope for a new day
She sets this one for beauty
but she'll gladly take peace
She moves through the day
sometimes aware
sometimes numb
That has got to change
Slowly life becomes real
Her senses at ease
Calmed into the night
Open and waiting
she slips back to rest
Now, going to sleep is easy

Reunion of Spirits

It won't be like this forever
This distance that we feel
Each day brings us closer
to a reunion of our spirits
We need the presence of love
Acceptance is a strong high
Our conversions endless
Hopes and dreams shared
Someday it won't matter
when or where we meet
Our stories fill the time
Never wanting to return
to the usual beats of life
We encourage each other
through rough thoughts
It doesn't make sense
this bond we've created
We tried to let it go but
some forces can't be destroyed
Time and distance elusive
when we play with our souls
At this moment
we only have words
Soon we will have memories
once again to smile upon

Body of Strength

Water pours down my body
hydrating head to toe
soft and supple skin
Lathering hands smooth over
scrapes, bumps, and scars
My blemished badges of honor
Creamy suds slide over curves
weak and weary at times
Stretched beyond limits
creating miracles of life
Waiting to feel its beauty return
My hands glide lovingly
over beautiful imperfections
Love it gently and tenderly
like no one else ever will
Perfectly flawed figure
Body of Strength

Laura Serratos

Sweet Red

Sweet red clings to the rim
        ready for pink parted lips
A smooth flow of fruit
        awakens a tongue to life
A warm cascade of love
        gushes through a tunnel
        in fragrant splashes
My heart beats in rhythm
        with the sensation of desire
Another sip is waiting
        to join this delicious dance
Calm my fears instantly
        in unison cheers
Toast of the night
        sweet vine turned liquid lust

Warm Love

A stream of warm love
pours over my body
    "We're alone again
        just the way I like it"
I touch you with my hands
in all the right places
Silky smooth lather
tenderly flows over me
with tropical scents
Shimmery soft bubbles
drip down my damp skin
Like an ocean of waves
rinse away the day
Our time here is precious
we get lost in a mist
of steamy, soft suds
    "Let's make it last
        a little longer"
The flow is warm
My thoughts are clear

Hidden Strength

These marks upon her body
        tell the story of a woman's days
Her breasts marked for eternity
Swelled to nourish hunger and
strength to growing life

Laces of soft, pink ribbons
        tell a tale of war within,
        an invasion of the womb
She grows to provide safety
        for occupants taking up space
        who left that place happy
She cleans up for the next
        but skin is beyond repair
Nothing can sooth the scars
        hidden from the world

Only she sees the reminders
        of the capacity her body held
        with slashes of pure love
Maternal power stretched
        beyond the limits of strength
Her forever badge of glory

Morning Sky

The sky a blushing blue
amid cold, crisp air
It sends a chill through me,
exhilaration in my lungs

The morning dark and deep
like an ocean in the sky
Quiet, perfect stillness

Flicker of light from nearby windows
tell of life coming awake
I wonder if they feel it, too
the calm beauty of the dark
morning sky

The best time of day
stare out the window and
let your mind wander
soar with possibilities

Light breaks through now
with contrasting hues of blue
revealing more than I care to see

Let The Pen Lead

Just let it flow
Write whatever comes to mind
You don't need a fancy technique
Let the pen lead

Just let the feelings inside
pour out in the form of ink
like your blood dripping
from your artist's heart
The paper waiting to feel
a warm flow of thoughts,
feelings, and emotions

Let the noise drive you to
push harder to find the hidden ideas
Silence does not serve you

Just let it flow
from your hand
Don't be afraid that nothingness
will consume your senses
Time to release the fears
that keep within your head

Just let it flow
Let the paper capture
your stream of mind

Pulse of Pain

My head is pounding
I feel like I woke up twice
My dream was disturbing
Thoughts in my mind are making
me feel low and vulnerable
I should have been stronger
Last night, when I entered into
the subconscious, too many negative feelings took control

The pressure on my head is growing
Every pulse of pain reminds me
of what I don't want to think about
If I'm going to turn this day around
I need to clear my head

My body is heavy
I need to smooth out choppy thoughts
I feel unworthy
I'm holding back fear
Maybe I'll just let it out but
closing my eyes won't blind the pain
I just need to get back to
thoughts of power within

Laura Serratos

Smashing Train

There's just too much running
through my head right now
to try to make sense and write
Scenes and details
actions that are not clear
A picture I don't want to see
I try to reason it away
The image consumes my mind
I can't put it on paper
I can't give it a voice
It flows through my veins
It beats in my heart
It pours through my tears
I have no right to feel this way
It keeps coming with force
The impact will be
a smashing train
whistle screeching
From my lungs
glass and steel
burst from my mind
I'm a beautiful wreck

Total Silence

There's only ringing in my ears
A flame dances
bending and bowing in my presence
A sweet scent fills me
I want to relax into its light
The air is clear as my mind
The beauty that I see from
where I sit brings me
to question
if everyone has
a moment of deep wonder
Am I alone in silence?
Does anyone else hear the buzzing?
A creek in the floor
A snap at the window
There is no such thing as
total silence
in my reality

Laura Serratos

Watching Rainbows

Last night, my inner child
reminded me of my
hopes and dreams
      I will not deny her any longer
      I will let her come out and play
We sat together watching rainbows
We listened to Judy fill our ears with songs
of love and wonder

This little girl wants to be free
She reminded me of what the delicate
mind of an eight year old can dream
She's been waiting to feel those old
      beliefs of joy for a future out of reach
      seen and not heard for too long
She can help me feel again what a young
imagination and vision brings
A purpose to a boring existence
She needs to come out and sit with me
      I'll let her pick the song
      I'll let her choose the movie
Her pure loving innocence
is just what I need to make
desire a reality

A Simple Thought

I am loving the process
of working on myself
I love changing the mindset
Stunted for so many years
I think about who I could have been
Knowing what I know now
But that does not matter
The present moment is where I am
I am...
Such a simple thought, yet
the key to a new me
        Up or down
                Left or right
It is up to me to decide the direction
Too much time and energy used up
on the inner destruction of my peace

I've stirred the power
inside of me
growing stronger every day
The moments I take which bring me closer
a better version
of the woman I want to share
Within myself and the world

Laura Serratos

To Be Alive

I feel lucky to be alive
        to experience all the magical
        events taking place
I look to the sky and I see
        amazing objects in the universe perhaps
        many will never see

Planets floating and existing

I'm small by comparison
        but I have power within my naked eye
        for things I've only seen in books

As the cosmos spin in the sky
        they teach me to align
        as I should, with my
hopes, dreams, and goals

I'm here on earth
        at the right time
        meant to witness beauty

I feel so lucky to be alive

Flurries of Thought

Snow flurries move with the wind
      just as thoughts in my head
In all directions these ice particles
      pass through the air
      searching for a place to land

It's the same with my thoughts
They want to land and keep cold
      to freeze memories from my past
The crisp air gives them life
Just as bitter memories give life to emotions
      I wish I no longer lived

But a ray
      of hope, love, joy
      can melt away thoughts

Even the slightest bit of sun
on a glittery speck of icy water
has power to melt
fear, doubt, and sadness

Blind Faith

I'm going on blind faith
I've been thinking
      how things happen in life
sometimes you get what you need

A gentle nudge
Enough to get momentum going
A rough shove in the right direction
A hard push may make you
      trip and stumble along the way
But guess what?
      You're moving
Crawl, walk, run
Keep going in the direction of greatness
Have blind faith to see through the mess
It'll all make sense
      no time to stop
Your moment to shine is just ahead

Always Giving

I never imagined I was doing anything wrong
I am a giver
        of my time, talents, and treasure
I give with joy; it makes me feel good
Why is it so hard for me to receive?
Why do I say,
"I don't need…"
 or
"I don't want…"
tokens of appreciation
Do I not see myself as worthy?
Do I think everyone needs me more than I need them?

Yes, I am a giver
I want to receive, but
I draw back my appreciation and gratitude
I need to allow love in
to let love pour out
My spirit desires balance
So I say,
"Thank you" from my heart

Laura Serratos

Ancestor Woman

Who has gone before me?
Can I see her reflection in me?

A thought in an ancestor woman's mind

Did she think of me often?
Was she sad to never know me?
    My skin, my hair, my body

A brown, braided woman
    her mind on daily life
Could she perceive who I would be?
Did she bless my future?

Who will go after me?
A great, great, great, granddaughter
    on this earth without me
I long to teach her love
    her beauty from within
The strength of many women
    before I am a spark in the sky

Who has gone before me?
I never knew existed
I mourn for the love and life
    of a woman in my flesh and blood
I celebrate a woman who will
    one day wonder about me

Flight of a Duck

If I had to do it all again,
    would I make a change?

A duck flies above me
    in the snowy, morning sky
Does he think about starting over?
Would he go back and fly
    in the same direction?
Would he choose a different fish
    to satisfy his hunger?
No, this duck relies on instinct
    what calls him by nature

I search to find my purpose
Would I be here now if I changed
    even one event?
Would I want to skip over
    the heartache and pain?

I'll never know the outcome of that path
    I had never taken

I just know
If I were not where I am now
    I would have missed that duck's flight
    and all the beautiful contemplations
    that trailed after him

Dark Tunnel

Look deep inside
Find the inner peace
I close my eyes
searching through glass
of a dark tunnel

Specks of blue light
flash around guiding
my attention and focus

The deeper I go,
a kaleidoscope of images
spin through this
vast empty space

I see reflections of memories
visible in the dark
Emotions pull my mind
in the direction of my heart

When I close my eyes
I hope to see angels
dancing on clouds
But I see a dark gallery
of noisy patterns

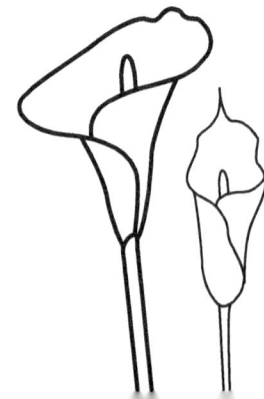

I, Too, Bloom

Laura Serratos

"Once the seed of poetry is planted in your heart, it's hard not to see life as anything other than poetic.
> Conversations are songs
> Thoughts are rhythms
> Experiences are inspirations

There's no going back!"

—Laura Serratos

Laura Serratos

The Effect

Instead of getting out of bed
I linger between the sheets with thoughts
Old notions of what others
once made me believe

It's like a game
where the pieces are stacked,
meant to fall on each other
creating a pattern
of self-doubt

I need all of my will power
Careful not to start the effect
by the slightest acceptance
of apathetic opinions

But just one powerful sweep
of love and strength
from my symbolic hand
send them crashing to the floor
I no longer desire to play

Tomorrow, I'll just get out of bed

Laura Serratos

Puzzle of Me

How do they fit together?
These awkward pieces of me
I started with the edges
That's the easiest way to begin
Filling in the middle takes time
Pieces of love and hate
can't interlock smoothly
Sometimes they're forced
but this never lasts
The right piece will come along

The image not yet clear
The original packaging destroyed
long before I had a chance to see

Time and experience
my only guidance
to make sense of it all
I'll just keep working at it
Every part laid out on the floor
Ready to be placed
What will make it whole?
This thousand piece
puzzle of me

Alone

My alarm goes off
I'm trying to affirm
my subconscious mind
then you come in out of nowhere

The night has become
my favorite time
I get to redo the damage

I'm aware of you now
and I want to fill you
with love and strength

I love seeing you before bed
The time I am most excited
to talk to you
tell you every night how I feel

We're alone and it feels good
to say what you need to hear

I cried and obsessed
but now I care for you
and only want to give
the best of my soul

Familiar Roads

This familiar road
I've driven a thousand times
      "Where are we going?'
I ask you
      "You already know"
You say

Travelling at a speed
where dust and rocks
Become a cloud around us

Look at the sky
Flames pouring down
in shapes of airplanes
and my heart

It's just a dream on a familiar road

We Took a Chance

I never meant to start this
I didn't think it could be
It's more than I can bare

I want you gone
I don't want you to leave
Are you as confused as I?

Two hearts crossing roads of time and space
Trying to figure it out creates more confusion

I'm not a healer
if that's what you need
I offer my softness
Don't turn me to stone, please

Laura Serratos

Where's My Muse

I'm lacking inspiration

How can I write
when all I see
is my own backyard
Surroundings meant to free and save me
are now stifling my head

When I look at the sky
I want to see magic
Not a cloudy overcast on rooftops and sheds

Routine creates structure
but not for an artist's heart
I need to get away
I need some air to breathe

Life To Be Lived

She can barely get the words out
Her eyes tired from the day
Tears form in the corners of her eyes
with a yawn and stretched out lips
Tangled hair layered down her back

She thinks about her weary body
resting on a soft warm bed
It'll take her to her dreamworld
or maybe a chance to sleep
It feels good to lay down
After a long, makeup free day
But there's
- ☐ dinner to be cooked
- ☐ dishes to be washed
- ☐ puppies to be fed
- ☐ life to be lived
- ☐ words to be written

The day stuck in her mind
Needs to be released
to make room for tomorrow
when she starts over again.

Laura Serratos

Intentions

It's midnight
I can't sleep
I write my intentions
They bloom to life

I'm grounded
ready to bring beauty and good
into this awesome world
My intentions focused on love
A beacon of guiding light

Writing keeps my thoughts pure
Because I know the strength
of my words and intentions

Illogical Pain

Low vibrations
This feeling in my head
takes me to a place I once visited

A surge of pain through my chest
Tells me I'm going to be hurt again

Nothing helps settle my mind
muscles tense and tight
Trying to release tension
are heavy with worry
over things not meant to control

A single tear is all I allow
to burn my cheek
Gone with a flick of my finger
I'll pretend I feel nothing
Until there's nothing to feel

Illogical pain is not a birthright

Laura Serratos

Emotional Clouds

Left over emotional clouds,
      never cleared away,
           casts a shadow
on a once happy mind

Self-Love

As I close my eyes, I relax into
        a state of being
 I am present

My body is filled with warmth
The love of my guides
Surrounds me and fills my body
A stirring within

Caressed by soft air to my lungs
leaves this moment
rising with warmth inside

I am becoming one with the version
of the self who I truly love

Breathing new life into existence
        cleanses my mind and my spirit
A smile breaks free
my lips part
the tenderness of a kiss

I give to myself

Laura Serratos

The Power Within

A self-discovery journey
        a life of love and abundance

I can manifest without awareness

I am doing something special,
unaware of the real power inside of me

I am meant to create

I am confident
I can accomplish anything I set in my mind

New opportunities are flowing into my life
bringing good along my path

I am full of potential and my dreams are possible
I am a magnet for abundance and blessings
I am open and ready to receive from the beautiful universe
I visualize my dream life and watch it manifest into reality

I am powerful

January 20

This feeling that wells up in my chest
signals my true heart's desire
I can't ignore my intricate guiding system
pushing me in the direction
which explores the authentic road

I know where I want to be
and what I want to do

What is real about being boxed into a life
that does not emphasize the uniqueness
of my existence?

I have potential within
to change what no longer serves me

Late-Bloomer

The dirt was cracked
I began to sprout
Forty years buried under

It's alright
I'm doing just fine

You'll see my stems
Bulbs ready to burst
Soft pink petals
long to kiss the sun
Water my roots
Fertilize my stem
Don't pick me yet
I need to feel soil
Bees pollinate my skin
Cool breeze in the night
Moon beams caress me
I don't have much time
Let my beauty bloom
Butterflies massage my leaves
I sway to the breeze
Before I drop my seed

I'm a late-bloomer
as you can see
but I'm taking up

    T h e   S p a c e   I   N e e d

I, Too, Bloom

Bio

Laura Serratos is a Mexican American English Language Arts teacher, writer, author, and poet in Northwest Indiana. In 2003, Laura earned a B.A. in English and an M.Ed. in School Administration from Purdue University Calumet where she launched a website dedicated to highlighting the creative works of women in the arts. After spending some time as a substitute teacher, she received a Master of Arts in Teaching at Calumet College of St. Joseph. She has spent ten years in education where she has been touched tremendously by the lives and stories of her students who come from all walks of life, which often inspire her written work.

At a very young age, Laura knew that one day she would see her name in the title of her own book. Many weekends were spent at her grandparent's home in the South Chicago neighborhood where her imagination took off. Armed with paper, markers, and a stapler, the seed of authorship was planted in the heart of a young eight year old girl. Laura dreamed of one day telling her story of love, laughter, and the sometimes hard realities of life. A bit of this dream has been fulfilled with an original piece published within a student anthology at the University of Illinois at Chicago, where she completed some undergraduate work.

Laura Serratos lives in Schererville, Indiana with her husband, four children, baby Jude and furbabies, Penny and Reader. When she is not teaching and writing, you could find her engrossed in poetry, fiction or self-help. More important hobbies include travelling to discover food and culture, wishing upon a star, and staring out of the window daydreaming about rainbows and butterflies.

Acknowledgements

I want to thank the following people who have over the years contributed in some way to making this book a reality:

To my husband, Sergio, for his understanding and support over the last seven months.

To my daughters, Carissa, Christa, and Caralyna, for helping to keep the pups quiet on Tuesday nights.

To my son, Christopher, and Cathy for giving me the best reason to make this project successful, my grandson, baby Jude.

To my mother, Gloria, for always being proud of all the accomplishments her family achieves, big and small.

To my grandparents, father, brothers, sisters-in-law, aunts, uncles, cousins, niece and nephews, you have all shaped who I am in some way.

To my mentor, Davina Ferreira, whose encouragement and faith in my creativity has led me to my inner artist. You are true inspiration.

To my Alegria family, who will always be a part of my heart and soul. You have all helped me bloom. We are forever bonded by a love of writing and poetry.

To anyone who has ever confided in me by sharing your story, courage, and strength. Thank you for your trust.

Finally, to the reader, for it is you who gives life to my thoughts and words.

Laura Serratos

www.ingramcontent.com/pod-product-compliance
Lightning Source LLC
Chambersburg PA
CBHW072203100526
44589CB00015B/2348